OVERHEAD THE SUN

Lines from Walt Whitman

OVERHEAD THE SUN

Woodcuts by Antonio Frasconi

Farrar, Straus and Giroux

New York

Copyright © 1969 by Antonio Frasconi. All rights reserved

Library of Congress catalog card number: 69-20284

PRINTED IN THE UNITED STATES OF AMERICA

Published simultaneously in Canada by Doubleday Canada Ltd., Toronto

First edition, 1969

Beginning my studies the first step pleas'd me so much,
The mere fact consciousness, these forms, the power of
     motion,
The least insect or animal, the senses, eyesight, love,
The first step I say awed me and pleas'd me so much,
I have hardly gone and hardly wish'd to go any farther,
But stop and loiter all the time to sing it in ecstatic songs.

from Inscriptions : Beginning My Studies

Lo, the unbounded sea,
On its breast a ship starting, spreading all sails, carrying
     even her moonsails,
The pennant is flying aloft as she speeds she speeds so
     stately — below emulous waves press forward,
They surround the ship with shining curving motions
     and foam.

from Inscriptions : The Ship Starting

This then is life,
Here is what has come to the surface after so many
      throes and convulsions.

How curious! how real!
Underfoot the divine soil, overhead the sun.

from Starting from Paumanok

Afoot and light-hearted I take to the open road,
Healthy, free, the world before me,
The long brown path before me leading wherever I choose.

*

Now I see the secret of the making of the best persons,
It is to grow in the open air and to eat and sleep with the earth.

from Song of the Open Road

There was a child went forth every day,
And the first object he look'd upon, that object he became,
And that object became part of him for the day or a certain
    part of the day,
Or for many years or stretching cycles of years.

from There Was a Child Went Forth

To me the sea is a continual miracle,
The fishes that swim — the rocks — the motion of the waves
    — the ships with men in them,
What stranger miracles are there?

from Autumn Rivulets : Miracles

I stand as on some mighty eagle's beak,
Eastward the sea absorbing, viewing, (nothing but sea
    and sky,)
The tossing waves, the foam, the ships in the distance,
The wild unrest, the snowy, curling caps—
    that inbound urge and urge of waves,
Seeking the shores forever.

from Sands at Seventy : From Montauk Point

I have not so much emulated the birds that musically
     sing,
I have abandon'd myself to flights, broad circles.
The hawk, the seagull, have far more possess'd me
     than the canary or mocking-bird,
I have not felt to warble and trill, however sweetly,
I have felt to soar in freedom and in the fullness of power,
     joy, volition.

from Old Age Echoes : To Soar in Freedom and in Fullness of Power

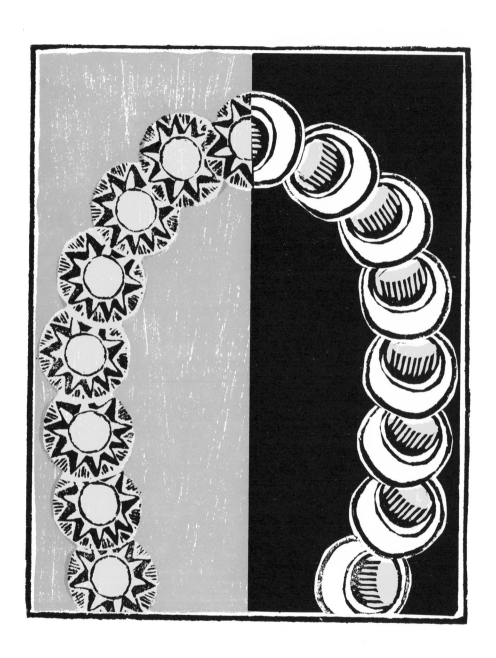

Day full-blown and splendid — day of the immense sun,
     action, ambition, laughter,
The Night follows close with millions of suns,
     and sleep and restoring darkness.

from Youth, Day, Old Age and Night

Long and long has the grass been growing,
Long and long has the rain been falling,
Long has the globe been rolling round.

from Song of the Exposition

A song of the rolling earth, and of words according,
Were you thinking that those were the words,
    those upright lines? those curves, angles, dots?
No, those are not the words, the substantial words are
    in the ground and sea,
They are in the air, they are in you.

from A Song of the Rolling Earth

Simple and fresh and fair from winter's close emerging,
As if no artifice of fashion, business, politics,
    had ever been,
Forth from its sunny nook of shelter'd grass —
    innocent, golden, calm as the dawn,
The spring's first dandelion shows its trustful face.

from Sands at Seventy : The First Dandelion

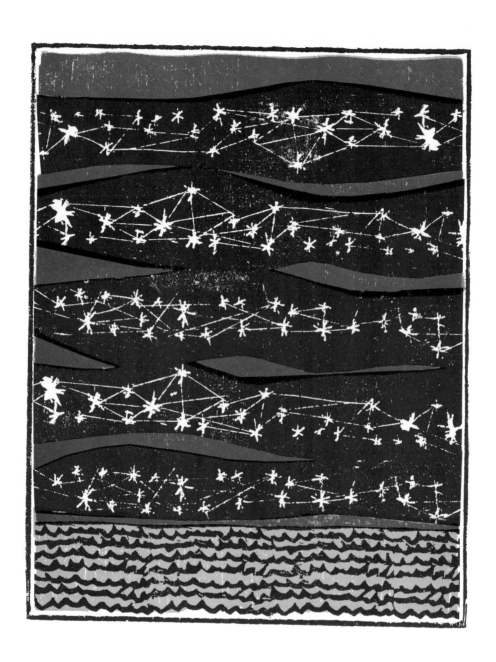

On the beach at night alone,
As the old mother sways her to and fro singing her husky
    song,
As I watch the bright stars shining, I think a thought of the
    clef of the universes and of the future.

from Sea-Drift : On the Beach at Night Alone

When lilacs last in the dooryard bloom'd,
And the great star early droop'd in the western sky
    in the night,
I mourn'd, and yet shall mourn with ever-returning spring.

from Memories of President Lincoln:
    When Lilacs Last in the Dooryard Bloom'd

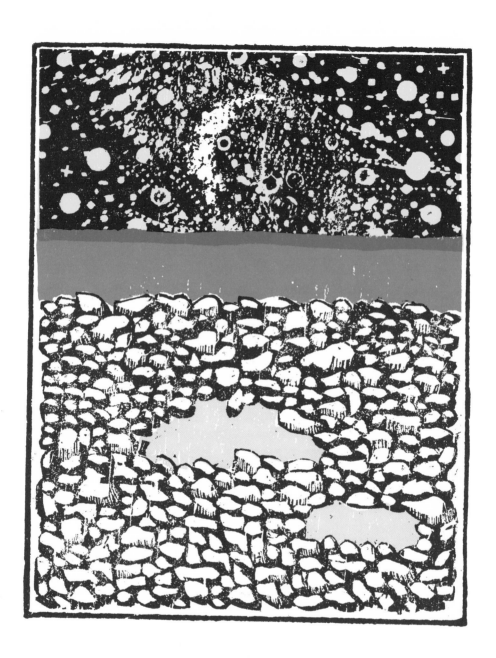

On the beach at night,
Stands a child with her father,
Watching the east, the autumn sky.

Up through the darkness,
While ravening clouds, the burial clouds,
　　in black masses spreading,
Lower sullen and fast athwart and down the sky,
Amid a transparent clear belt of ether yet left in the east,
Ascends large and calm the lord-star Jupiter,
And nigh at hand, only a very little above,
Swim the delicate sisters the Pleiades.

from Sea-Drift: On the Beach at Night

In cabin'd ships at sea,
The boundless blue on every side expanding,
With whistling winds and music of the waves, the large
        imperious waves,
Or some lone bark buoy'd on the dense marine

from Inscriptions: In Cabin'd Ships at Sea

Hand-set in Emerson type at THE SPIRAL PRESS · NEW YORK

Printed by CRAFTON GRAPHIC COMPANY, INC · NEW YORK

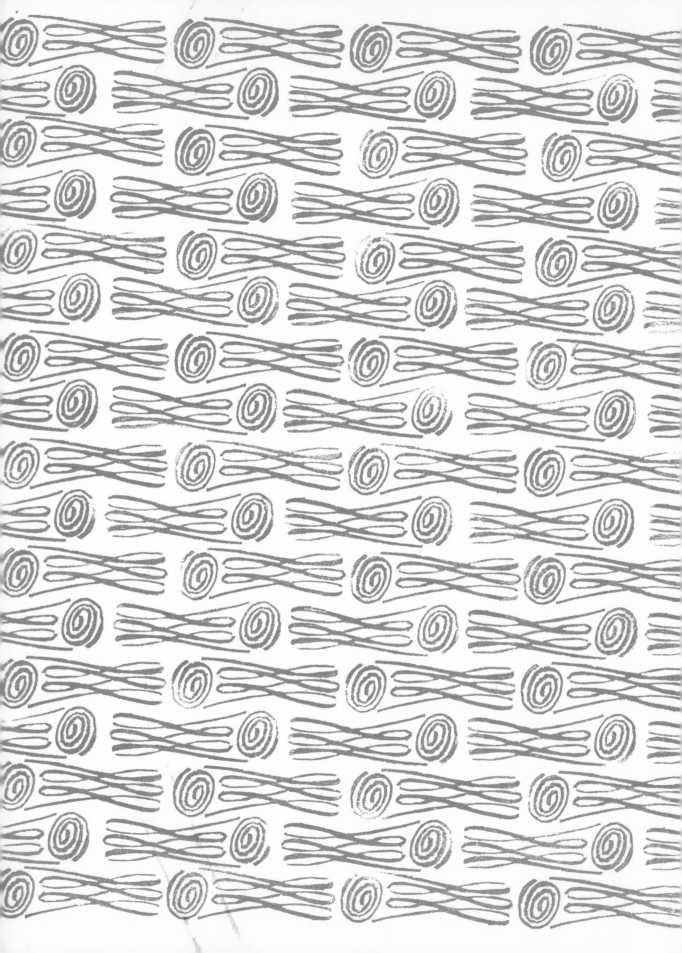